61 Latera

Puzzles

The Entry-Level Logic and Riddle Book Designed for Family After-Dinner Activities

Karen J. Bun

Bluesource And Friends

This book is brought to you by Bluesource And Friends, a happy book publishing company.

Our motto is **"Happiness Within Pages"**

We promise to deliver amazing value to readers with our books.

We also appreciate honest book reviews from our readers.

Connect with us on our Facebook page www.facebook.com/bluesourceandfriends and stay tuned to our latest book promotions and free giveaways.

Don't forget to claim your FREE books!

Brain Teasers:

https://tinyurl.com/karenbrainteasers

Harry Potter Trivia:

https://tinyurl.com/wizardworldtrivia

Sherlock Puzzle Book (Volume 2)

https://tinyurl.com/Sherlockpuzzlebook2

Also check out our other books

"67 Lateral Thinking Puzzles"

https://tinyurl.com/thinkingandriddles

"Rookstorm Online Saga"

https://tinyurl.com/rookstorm

"Korman's Prayer"

https://tinyurl.com/kormanprayer

"The Convergence"

https://tinyurl.com/bloodcavefiction

"The Hardest Sudokos In Existence (Ranked As The Hardest Sudoku Collection Available In The Western World)"

https://tinyurl.com/MasakiSudoku

Table of Contents

BLUESOURCE AND FRIENDS 2

INTRODUCTION 6

61 LATERAL THINKING PUZZLES 10

SOLUTIONS TO ALL PUZZLES 41

CONCLUSION 55

Introduction

Thank you for purchasing *61 Lateral Thinking Puzzles: The Entry Level Logic and Riddle Book Designed for Family After-Dinner Activities.* If you are reading this, then you are in store for a lot of fun and brain teasing.

In this book, you will find a collection of word problems, riddles, and puzzles which are sure to pique your interest, and put your brainpower to the test. Now, these aren't just any ordinary brain teasers. These are logic-based puzzles, where you will have to test your understanding and knowledge of the information provided in the puzzle, along with your own knowledge and abilities.

These puzzles are a great way to stimulate conversation among friends and family. They make for great dinner conversations, especially when you are looking to mix things up a bit. These puzzles are sure to give your brain a good workout.

Please keep in mind that these puzzles do have correct answers. So, it is important to work through your conversation in order to get the right answer. In addition, it is best to develop a strategy to figure out the final answer.

For you to get the most out of this book, here are some helpful suggestions and ideas that can help you maximize the benefits that you can get while completing each of the puzzles.

First of all, one great way to go about this strategy is to jot down your ideas. You can have a brainstorming session where everyone gets a chance to present their ideas. Then, you can talk about the answer that you believe makes the most sense. Finally, you can vote on the best one. This approach works really well when you are in a group setting, especially if there is a large number of people.

Now, if you are on your own, it is always helpful to think out loud. Often, hearing yourself say something can help put things into perspective. That allows you to assess the solution that you have come up with.

Moreover, the most important thing to bear in mind is that as long as you maintain a collaborative effort, you can always find a good solution to each of the puzzles contained in this collection. Of course, two heads think better than one. So, the same goes for multiple heads. Fostering collaborative effort in solving each one of these puzzles is a great way to build trust and stimulate cooperation among family members, friends, and colleagues.

Another useful tip is to have a lead. Now, this is not so much a leader, but a lead or moderator to keep order in the conversation. The lead can make sure that everyone gets their turn to speak. That way, no one will get left out. The main purpose of having a leader is to guide the discussion so that participants do not veer off-topic. Furthermore, the lead can offer hints and helpful suggestions in case anyone gets stuck.

Leads ought to be the only ones with access to the solutions. This will take away the temptation to skip ahead and check out what the solution is. That way, each team will have to figure out their own solution(s) to each one of the puzzles in a creative fashion.

Another spin on this could be a more competitive approach. This approach works great if you have a large number of people at your gathering. The total number of participants can be divided into two groups. The lead can act as a master of ceremony who will read the problem to both teams. Then, each team is given an allotted amount of time to solve the puzzle. Each team designates a spokesperson who explains their answer. The lead is in charge of making sure that the correct answer is revealed once the discussion portion is over.

In general terms, 10 minutes per puzzle is a good amount of time to discuss a puzzle. Unless the puzzle in unusually complex, 10 minutes should suffice. Most importantly, you want to make sure that both teams have enough time for a discussion. If you feel that more time is required, then, by all means, assign more time in 5-minute increments. Make sure you don't forget to keep to the time, though!

Now, a very important warning: In the back of this book, you will find the solutions to each one of the puzzles presented herein. Please resist the temptation to go back and check out the solution beforehand. That is why it is best for the moderator or leader to be the only one with the solution in their hands.

Otherwise, you may not be able to resist the temptation of checking out the answers before you have worked out all of the possible solutions.

It is certainly worth taking the time to work out all of the possible solutions to each puzzle. It might even be that you can come up with a better solution to a puzzle than the one offered. So, don't hold back. Who knows? You might be able to come up with an even better solution.

What that in mind, let's begin!

61 Lateral Thinking Puzzles

Instructions: Please read through each one of the puzzles presented. Then, work individually in pairs or in groups to work out the answer. Once you have come up with one, you can refer to the back of this book to check out the correct solution.

Also, using visuals such as a board, flipchart, or just a plain pen and paper will help you in working out the possible solutions to each problem. Often, using visuals will help you and your teammates get a better understanding of the problem and its possible solution(s).

Please keep in mind that there is only one answer to each puzzle. And while it is perfectly plausible to come up with more than one answer, each puzzle has been designed to have just one logical solution.

Just a friendly reminder: Don't check the official answer until you have fully worked out the puzzle. If you check the answer before you have fully discussed the issue, you won't get the most out of the exercise.

So, without further ado, here we go!

Puzzle #1 The Twins Dilemma

A family happily welcomed their new twin sons. The boys were named Rory and Cory. After about a year, the parents realized something very strange. While they both have the same mother and the same father, and they were both born in the same city and in the same hospital, it turns out that Rory and Cory were born on a different day, month, and year.

How is this possible?

Puzzle #2 How Did the Farmer Cross the River?

A farmer is walking with a sheep, a wolf, and a sack of grain. When he gets to his boat to cross the river, the farmer realizes that the sheep, the wolf, and the grain, in addition to himself, would be too much weight for the boat. So, he can only take one of the sheep, wolf, and grain, along with himself in the boat and across the river.

Thus, he needs to take one by one across the river. However, here is the catch: If he leaves the sheep and the wolf alone, the wolf will eat the sheep. If he leaves the sheep and the grain alone, the sheep will eat the grain.

Oh, what should a farmer do?

How can the farmer get all three across the river?

Puzzle #3 Mr. Jones' Math Class

In a high school, there are three girls in Mr. Jones' math class: Mary, Cindy, and Josephine. Mary speaks more softly than Cindy, and Josephine speaks more loudly than Cindy. Since the girls talk too loudly in class, Mr. Jones has decided to punish all of the students, except for the students who speak the softest. Mary has said that she speaks the softest. Josephine disagrees.

So, does Mary speak softer or more loudly than Josephine?

Puzzle #4 Speaking of Math Class...

Mr. Jones' other math class took their midterms last week. After grading the math test, the average score of the students in the class is 6. Eight students scored 3 points, and the rest scored over 5 points. Assuming that the total score is 10 and 5 is a passing grade, what is the average score of all of the students who passed the test?

Puzzle #5 The Big Race in the City

The city has decided to organize a race to determine the city's fastest runner. The winner would go on to compete in the state championship. Since thousands of runners signed up, the city decided to hold elimination trials until the top four runners were left. They would then have one final heat to decide who would be the city champion.

The four runners in the competition were labeled: A, B, C, and D. As far as the results go, we know that C arrived right after B, and D arrived in between A and C.

Can you determine the order in which they crossed the finish line so that we can figure out who the city champion is?

Puzzle #6 Going on Vacation With the Bros

Six friends have decided to go on vacation together after a long semester at college. However, they can't all take the same means of transportation together as they can't afford to fly. So, they have chosen to travel in pairs on the same means of transportation. Alex won't be driving, as he will join Jack, who isn't flying. Andy is flying. Charlie is not traveling with Mike, who doesn't fly either.

Based on the previous information, can you determine what means of transportation Tom is taking?

Puzzle #7 A Family of Big Eaters

A family that lives in a quiet village has four dogs: Scout, Precious, Buddy, and Ace. Each dog is a big eater. After going over the family's budget, the parents were shocked to see how much they spend on dog food each month. So, the parents have decided to determine which dog eats the least. The dog that eats the least would stay home, while the other three would be up for adoption.

This is what they found out:

Ace eats more than Scout. Buddy eats more than Scout, but less than Precious. Precious eats more than Ace.

Which dog gets to stay home with the family?

Puzzle #8 To Shoplift or Not to Shoplift?

In a large department store, on a regular day, a woman enters, takes a shopping cart, and proceeds to fill it up to the top. Then, the lady walks out of the store without paying for anything, and without being stopped by the store's security guards. She was caught on the store's security cameras as well.

How is it possible that the lady can leave the department store without being stopped by security?

Puzzle #9 A Bit Too Much Excitement

A man is in a large, dark room having a great time. There is quite a bit of noise, but everyone is silent. Then, the man is unable to breathe or speak. The other people in the dark room do nothing help him, nor do they call for help. After a few moments, the man can breathe and speak again. He resumes having a great time, along with everyone else.

How is this situation possible?

Puzzle #10 Tell Me What You See

A local bookstore has offered free, premium memberships to its book club for the first 10 customers who successfully crack a code.

The question posed by the bookstore was:

Please look at the following image.

You have 10 seconds to indicate what it means.

Based on this information, can you solve the puzzle, and give the answer to the bookstore's customers?

Puzzle #11 Which Way Is Up?

A man lives in the penthouse of a 45-story building in a large, metropolitan city. The man is very fit and athletic. He has a great job. In the mornings, he leaves home at 7:45 and takes the elevator down to the lobby of this apartment building. However, he takes the stairs up every evening when he gets home at around 7 pm.

Why does the man take the elevator down in the morning but not up in the evening?

Puzzle #12 Going Around in Circles

A very well-respected lawyer works in a fancy office building downtown. Every morning, when she gets to her office, she needs to drive around in circles six times before she can park her car, and then proceed to make her way to her office. Sometimes, other cars are blocking her way around in circles.

Why does she have to drive around in circles every day before parking and going to her office?

Puzzle #13 That's All She Wrote

A very wealthy lady sits at her desk every month and writes two words on 60 pieces of paper every week. The pieces of paper are small but important. She must do this every week as many people are counting on her to do so.

Why would this lady write two words on 60 pieces of paper every week?

Puzzle #14 Swing and a Miss

During a baseball game, the best batter on the team has two strikes. There are no runners on the bases. On the next pitch, the batter swings and misses, thereby striking out. The batter then scrambles toward first base. He reaches first base and is called "safe" by the umpire.

So, why isn't the batter out and standing at first base?

Puzzle #15 Burning the Candle at Both Ends

Rob is a very hard worker. He's got a steady job with steady hours. So, he is happy that he has a respectable job. He has a nice family, and enjoys fishing when he gets the chance to go. He usually stays up all night. He doesn't get any sleep at all at night, but does not end up feeling exhausted in the morning. He does this on a regular basis.

How is it possible that Rob doesn't sleep at night, yet he is not exhausted in the morning?

Puzzle #16 Child's Play

There are several children playing in the playground. Two kids are in the sandbox, playing quietly on their own. One child has made 3 sand piles, and the other child has made 4 sand piles. Then, one of the kids starts talking to the other one. Both children decide that they want to make a large sandcastle. So, they figure out that the best way to make a large sandcastle is to combine their piles.

After combining their sand piles to make their castle, how many piles do they have?

Puzzle #17 Your Wishes Are My Command

There was once a very powerful wizard. This wizard could grant any wishes and desires. After a very long life, the wizard felt he was about to die. So, he called his faithful servant in his chamber. The wizard said to his servant, "My dear servant, you have served me faithfully over all of these years. I feel that I will soon leave this life. As a reward for your faithful service, I will grant you one wish".

The wizard gave his servant one day to think about this wish. So, the servant went home to his wife and told him about this. Since this couple had been childless, his wife urged him to ask his master for a child.

Then, the servant went to see his mother, who had lost her sight. After telling his mother about what his master had offered, his mother asked him to request for her sight back.

On his way back from seeing his mother, the servant thought about what he wanted. He decided that he wanted to be very rich. He decided that he wanted a lot of money to solve all of his worries.

The next day, the wizard called his servant. "My dear servant, have you decided what wish you desire?"

The servant then made one wish where he was able to get all three desires.

How is it possible to get all three wishes into a single wish?

Puzzle #18 Something's Fishy

A lovely elderly lady had a beautiful blue tropical fish. She loved this fish dearly, as it was her only companion. One day, she noticed that the fish was swimming about strangely and seemed to be sick. Since this was her beloved companion, the lady rushed her fish to the vet.

The vet took one look at the fish and said, "Come back in an hour."

The lady smiled and nodded. She left and then came back in an hour to see her beloved companion swimming around happily and healthily. She was ecstatic about the miraculous turnaround. When she asked the vet what was wrong, all he said was,

"He just needed some fish medicine," that's all.

How was the vet able to achieve this seemingly miraculous recovery in such a short period of time?

Puzzle #19 Final Destination for Bobby

Bobby had no parents. One day, his guardian decided that he could no longer afford to take care of him. So, the guardian decided to send him away to live in the country with relatives of his. Since the guardian had to work, he could not accompany Bobby on the train ride to the country. In addition, Bobby could not read nor write. So, the guardian placed a large label around Bobby's neck with Bobby's name and the address to where he was meant to go. Despite the fact that the railway staff was very helpful, Bobby never made it to his final destination.

Why didn't Bobby make it to his final destination?

Puzzle #20 Someone Had to Draw the Line

A research unit at a prestigious university wanted to test a group of people's perception skills. To this end, the researchers crafted a test in which they would evaluate their test subjects' skills. The test consisted of a single item that read this way:

Please observe the following image.

Now, please respond to the following question:

Can you determine which of the two lines is longer?

Puzzle #21 Swinging for the Fences

A farmer has a large field which is surrounded by a fence. In his field, the farmer has a barn with six horses inside. One night, the six horses were inside the barn. Then, lightning struck, and the sound of thunder spooked three of the horses. They busted through the barn door and ran outside. The other three horses stayed inside the safety of the barn.

Since the farmer was fast asleep after a long day of work, he didn't notice the lightning strike. In the morning, he went about his usual routine with all six horses.

How is this possible?

Puzzle #22 An Unusual Meal

A very large and crowded restaurant was bustling at lunchtime. It was a pleasant afternoon until Billy entered the restaurant. As soon as Billy entered, all of the customers in the restaurant left their meals, got up from their tables, and hurried out the door as soon as possible. No one even bothered to pay for their meals, much less ask for the check.

Why did the customers of this restaurant flee as soon as they saw Billy enter?

Puzzle #23 Where's the Dough?

An old miser walks into a bank. He walks up to the window and indicates to the teller that he is there to withdraw all the money from his account. The teller complies and gives the man all of the money in his account. The man then counts his money and asks the teller to deposit the money back into his account.

Why would the miser withdraw the money, count it, and then deposit it back into his account?

Puzzle #24 Going for a Ride

On one occasion, a married couple wanted to go on a vacation. When they went about booking their seat on the flight, the airline wanted to charge the wife extra, since she was so big and needed more than one seat. At the same time, the husband insisted that he shouldn't be charged the full fare for his seat, as he didn't take up the whole seat.

After some haggling back and forth, the airline agreed to charge the married couple for two regular seats even though the wife needed more than one and the husband didn't even take up the entire seat.

Why did the airline end up charging the married couple for just the two seats?

Puzzle #25 Paying the Price

A young college student walks to a counter. She talks to the man behind the counter and places a book on the counter. The man looks at the book and then tells the young lady,

"That will be five dollars, please."

The young lady places a five-dollar bill on the counter. The man takes it, and she begins to walk away. The young lady leaves the book on the counter. She does not go back for it, nor does the man call the young lady to come back for it. The young lady did not return to get the book at any time.

Why did the lady pay for the book but not take it with her?

Puzzle #26 Not Buying It

After a long day at work, Jimmy had dinner, and then decided to watch television. Around midnight, his local television station broadcast a weather update:

"The current rainstorm will continue for another two days. Please make sure to take the necessary precautions to ensure your safety. On the bright side, it will be warm and sunny in 72 hours."

Jimmy scoffed at the weather forecast and muttered:

"They got that one wrong yet again."

If the rain will continue for two more days, but then will become warm and sunny in 72 hours, how could the forecast be wrong?

Puzzle #27 Life is a Game

Henry is a young boy who wants to play video games all day and do nothing else. He doesn't want to go to school nor do his homework.

One day, Henry's father warned Henry that if he didn't get his act together, he would take away his video game console. Henry pleaded with his dad not to take away his console. Henry's father agreed that he could keep the console in his room, but if he didn't shape up, he would be unable to play with it anyway.

Sure enough, Henry didn't shape up. As per the promise, Henry's father left the console in Henry's room. He left the console intact, and he did not remove any of its components. Henry's father managed to solve the problem using a hammer and some good, old-fashioned elbow grease.

So, how is it possible that Henry's father left the console in his room, intact, but used a hammer to make it impossible for Henry to play with it?

Puzzle #28 I Dare You

Mike and Joe are drinking on a Saturday afternoon in Mike's apartment, which is 15 stories up. After some drinks, Joe's friend dares him to jump out of a window to prove he can do this without being injured.

Mike accepts the dare, proceeds to jump out of the window, and lands harmlessly on the street below.

How can Mike go through the dare without being hurt?

Puzzle #29 What Are You Up To?

Following a crime spree, where a man had been spotted shoplifting several times, the police decided to put up "wanted" posters all over the town. The police had been able to identify the man's face clearly as security cameras had captured his image. Witnesses had also identified the man seen in the security camera footage.

One day, two police officers saw this man. They were well aware that this man was a famous criminal. But, they did nothing to arrest him.

If the two police officers had seen this man who had been clearly identified as the robber, why didn't they do anything to arrest him?

Puzzle #30 It's Completely Puzzling…

A group of research students wanted to test the math skills of another group of students. The research students were looking to stump their counterparts to measure their ability to deal with complex issues. So, they devised the following exercise. Here are the instructions:

Please have a look at this number puzzle.

2	11	20
4	9	32
7	8	49
4	10	?

Now, please find the missing number. There is only *one* correct answer.

So, what do you think is the missing number?

Puzzle #31 Empty Space

Three men are walking together on the street. They enter into an empty building together, on foot, at the same time. After some time inside the building, the night watchman came in to find the building completely empty. The footage on the security cameras showed the men walking into the building, but not walking out.

What happened to the three men who entered the building when the watchman found the building to be completely empty?

Puzzle #32 Dude, I Can't Open the Door!

After a night of partying, a young man arrives home at his apartment. As he arrives at his front door, he finds that he is unable to open the door. Confused, he makes sure that he's got the right building. *Yes, he's got the right building.* Also, he makes sure that he's got the right apartment number on the right floor. *Check.* He was even greeted by one of his neighbors who offered to help.

This man struggled for a few more minutes before giving up. He sat down outside his door and passed out.

Why couldn't this man enter his apartment?

Puzzle #33 What a Pile Up

On a calm, sunny day, there were a large number of cars that crashed into each other. About 30 cars, trucks, and even buses were involved in the pile-up. There were even some military vehicles involved in the pile-up of cars. Most of the vehicles had been overturned. Some had been flung a long distance from the initial point of impact. Yet, no ambulances were at the scene, and no police arrived. No one was injured. There was no commotion and no reports in the news. Most importantly, no people were harmed as a result of this pile-up.

Why was the scene so calm despite the large pile-up of vehicles?

Puzzle #34 Whacky Weather

Joe was driving down the road on a bright, sunny day. Then, he came to a full stop and eased up slowly before it suddenly got dark. He had to roll up his windows as water began pouring all around his car. Next, the water stopped just as suddenly as it had begun. After that, a gust of wind enveloped the car. Finally, the sun came back out, and the man was able to continue his trip safely.

How are these sudden changes in condition possible?

Puzzle #35 Are You Lion to Me?

On a very warm Saturday afternoon, a woman was walking down a path. Suddenly, she spotted a roaring lion in the distance. The lion started running in her direction, yet the woman was unafraid and did not make any effort to flee. She seemed to be completely at ease upon the sight of the lion.

Why didn't the woman flee when she saw the roaring lion running in the distance?

Puzzle #36 A Letter to the Editor

A faithful reader of a local newspaper decided to write a letter to the editor, hoping to get her letter published in the Sunday edition of the paper. This is what she wrote:

Dear Editor,

Can you respond to the following question?

What can be found once in a minute, twice in a moment, but never found in a hundred years?

Sincerely,

Martha Smith

What do you think the editor's reply to this letter was?

Puzzle #37 The Hitchhiker's Tale

A hitchhiker is standing in the pouring rain. There are plenty of cars passing by, but no one stops to offer the man a ride. Finally, after quite some time in the rain, a car slowly passed by with its emergency lights flashing. As the car slows down further, the hitchhiker runs up to it, open up one of the car doors and jumps in. As he is clearing the rain from his eyes, he notices that there is no driver, yet the car is still moving. The hitchhiker begins to call out, but no one replies. Freaking out, he decides to open the door and jump out of the car. He lands safely on the street and runs away.

How is it possible for the car to be moving without anyone driving it?

Puzzle #38 Some Legalese for You

At a big law conference, the top lawyers in the country gathered for their annual meeting. The organizers decided to hold a contest to test the knowledge of the conference attendees. One of the questions posed during the contest was the following:

Did you know that there is one type of crime which is punishable by law if it is attempted, but is not punishable if actually committed? What crime are we talking about?

A very young lawyer immediately raised her hand and gave the correct answer.

What did she answer?

Puzzle #39 Mind your Ps and Qs

Here is a question that was part of a contest run by a local newspaper. The prize for the right answer was a free monthly subscription. Here is the question:

This particular word has 6 total letters. The 2nd, 4th, and 6th letters are the same. If you skip 7 letters, starting from the first letter, you get the 3rd letter. And if you skip 7 letters again, starting from the 3rd, then you get the 5th letter.

Can you determine what word we are talking about?

Puzzle #40 Tunnel Vision

Please look at the following image:

Now, here is the situation:

A truck wishing to enter this tunnel is one inch too high. Thus, it will get stuck if it attempts to make its way through the tunnel. There is no other way of reaching its destination aside from going through this tunnel. The driver must be at his destination in one hour, and has little time to spare.

What can the driver do to fit in the tunnel?

Puzzle #41 Now that You Mention It

Speaking of trucks, a police officer saw a truck driver going the wrong way on a one-way street. The street was clearly marked as one-way. But, the police officer said nothing to the driver and let him go on his way.

Why didn't the police officer do anything about the driver going the wrong way on a one-way street?

Puzzle #42 Color Me...

An old man decided to go live on his own in the wilderness. He wanted to get away from civilization to have the best possible view of the world. In the place he chose, he built a rectangular house, but given the location, he could only see south from any of the four corners of his new house. Then one day, he saw a bear pass by the front of his home.

What color was the bear that passed by?

Puzzle #43 Making the Grade

The teacher of a fifth-grade class was told that the school superintendent would be stopping by for inspection some time the following week. The teacher was very concerned about giving a good impression of both himself and the students.

The school principal told the teacher that the superintendent would be asking questions to the children, but that the teacher would be allowed to choose who responded to each question. So, the teacher needed to figure out a way where he could be sure that the student he picked knows the right answer.

The day before the superintendent arrived, the teacher gave his students some instructions where he could be certain that he would always pick a student who knew the right answer.

What instructions did the teacher give his students?

Puzzle #44 The Fly in the Coffee

In a busy coffee shop, a lady sat down to get a cup of coffee. The waiter served her a cup and a bagel. After a few moments, the lady called the waiter over and said,

"There's a fly in my coffee."

The waiter nodded and said,

"My apologies, ma'am. I'll get you another cup."

A few moments later, the waiter arrived with another cup of coffee. The lady had a sip and said to the waiter,

"Hey! This is the same cup as the one with a fly in it!"

How did the lady know she had been served the same cup of coffee but without the fly?

Puzzle #45 The All-Black

A man is standing in the middle of the road. He is wearing an all-black costume. His face is covered by a black ski mask. He is wearing black gloves. All the buildings in the town are painted black. The tarmac is all black, with no stripe painted on it. The streetlights are also painted black. Then, a totally black car, with black tint on its windows approaches the man. The car has its headlights turned off. Just as the car is about to hit the man, the car turned and avoided the man.

How was the driver of the car able to identify the man right before hitting him?

Puzzle #46 A Job Interview

A company is looking to fill a vacancy for a top-level executive position. The interviewer is talking to several candidates. The position calls for someone who is exceptionally sharp and perceptive.

The last candidate to be interviewed, a tall, young lady, is sitting in a chair at the end of the table in a large conference room. The interview sits at the other end of the table. The interview places a cup of warm tea before the young lady but without the tea bag inside of it and far away from her so that she wouldn't be able to get a glimpse of the drink without getting up. The interviewer then asks the candidate,

"What's before you?"

To this question, the young lady immediately replies, without getting up,

"Tea."

The interviewer smiled and offered her the job on the spot.

How did the interviewer know this was the candidate he wanted?

Puzzle #47 At Opposite Ends

In a business meeting, two colleagues are sitting at opposite ends of the table. There is no one else sitting at the table. But, they cannot see each other. There is nothing on the table either, and there is nothing else that could be obstructing their view.

How is it that the two colleagues cannot see each other despite the absence of obstructions?

Puzzle #48 Home Alone

Imagine that you are home alone at night. The power has gone out, and there are no lights. Your only means of illumination are a candle, an oil lamp, and firewood. Then, you realize that you only have one match to light up these items.

What do you light up first?

Puzzle #49 Happy Birthday

As part of the final examination in a philosophy course, the professor asked the students in her class to answer the following question:

How many birthdays can a person have throughout the course of their life?

Only one of the students got the right answer.

What did he say?

Puzzle #50 Drawing the Line

In an advanced math class, the professor posed this challenge to his students.

Please look at the following image:

In the middle of this box, there is a line.

Now, how is it possible to make this line shorter without erasing it?

Puzzle #51 Order in the Court

The following case was brought before a judge at the local courthouse:

There was a petition by a man to marry his widow's sister.

After carefully studying the petition and reviewing applicable legislation, the judge proceeded to deny the petition.

Why did the judge deny the petition?

Puzzle #52 Driving me Crazy

You are an Uber driver in your city. Today is a really busy day. First, you pick up three passengers at Green Street, and drop them off at Main Avenue. Then, you pick up one passenger at Blue Road, and take him to Second Avenue. Finally, you pick up two more passengers on Red Street, and take them to the Gold building back on Main Avenue.

Now, what is the color of the driver's eyes?

Puzzle #53 A Man and his Daughters

Jennifer's dad, who is a retired military man, has five daughters. His first daughter is Mary, who is blonde. His second daughter is Peggy, who is a brunette. His third daughter is Debbie, who is also a blonde. His fourth daughter is Susie, who happens to be a redhead.

So, what is Jennifer's dad's fifth daughter's name?

Puzzle #54 A Traffic Jam

A city with a terrible traffic problem has decided to do something about it, finally. The city mayor has decided to restrict the circulation of vehicles by limiting the number of cars based on their color. As such, blue cars can circulate on Mondays and Wednesdays. Red cars can circulate on Tuesdays and Thursdays. Yellow cars can only circulate on the weekends. Green cars can circulate on Fridays. None of the car colors previously indicated may circulate on a day other than the day in which they have been authorized.

However, you can drive your car for any day of the week.

So, what color is your car?

Puzzle #55 At the Mercy of the Court

A convicted felon has been sentenced to death. After throwing himself at the mercy of the Court, the judge has decided to give the convicted one last opportunity to pardon his life. If he chooses correctly, the court will spare his life, though not his conviction.

The court gives the man the option to choose one of three doors.

The first door contains a raging blaze that the man must get through.

The second door contains three lions that haven't eaten in four years.

The third door contains a firing squad that is ready to fire.

To save his life, the felon must surpass the obstacles behind each door.

Which door does he choose?

Puzzle #56 Oh My Son!

A man and his son were driving down a long, deserted road. Suddenly, a large truck came out of nowhere, and struck the car. The man who was driving was tragically killed in the accident. The son, who was the passenger, was rushed to the hospital in serious condition.

Upon entering the hospital, the son was rushed into the operating room for emergency surgery. The surgeon on call immediately recognized the son and said,

"I cannot operate on my own son!"

How is this situation possible?

Puzzle #57 Challenge Me!

A local radio station has decided to run a challenge. The radio host challenged listeners to name three consecutive days without using the following days: Tuesday, Wednesday, or Saturday.

The winner of the challenge would receive a gift certificate of $500.

After numerous attempts, the tenth caller got the right answer.

What were the three consecutive days that beat the challenge?

Puzzle #58 Out the Window

A window washer was going about his daily routine. He was cleaning the windows on the 35th floor of a large office building. Suddenly, he slipped and fell. He was wearing no safety harness, and had no other protective gear. There was nothing to slow his fall, nor to cushion his landing. He fell to the floor with no other injuries, aside from a bruised ego.

How is this possible?

Puzzle #59 Make Sure You Study for the Test

An English professor decided to make his students' final course examination simple. He gave his students a single sheet of paper with a single question. The ones who got it right would pass the course. Those who didn't would fail. The entire course was riding on a single question.

This is the question:

What word in the English language, when four of its five letters are taken away, maintains the same pronunciation?

The students had two hours to solve the answer.

There is only one such word in the English language. What is it?

Puzzle #60 A Cat's Meow

A pet shop ran a contest directed at cat owners. The winner would receive a free lifetime supply (the cat's lifetime) of cat food. After unsuccessful attempts by multiple participants, an 8-year-old girl figured out the right answer.

Here is the question:

Which side of a cat has the most hair?

It took the little girl less than a minute to give the answer.

What answer did she give?

Puzzle #61 Do What You Will

A man decided to have his will written up. In it, he stated that, while he was from Hawaii, he wanted to be buried in Texas. When the lawyer read through his requests, the lawyer told the man that he could not be buried in Texas.

The will stated, "It is my will to be buried in Texas."

What reason did the lawyer give the man for not being able to be buried in Texas?

Congratulations on making it this far. You did a great job. You have certainly put in some hard work and brain power. Please remember that practice will help you get better in solving these types of puzzles. The more time you spend on these puzzles, the better you will become. In a way, it is just like going to the gym. But, with these exercises, you will be flexing your intellectual muscles!

Solutions to All Puzzles

In this section, you will find the solutions to each puzzle. Do take the time to go over each solution carefully. And, please remember, no cheating!

Puzzle #1 The Twins Dilemma

Solution: The twins' parents were relieved when they figured out that Rory was born on December 31st of one year at 11:59 pm, while Cory was born on January 1st of the next year at 12:01 am. Thus, they are identical twins and children of the same parents, but with completely different birthdays.

Puzzle #2 How Did the Farmer Cross the River?

Solution: The farmer must first take the sheep across, thereby leaving the wolf and the grain alone. Then, the farmer comes back for the wolf (or the grain) to take to the other side. Then, the farmer comes back across the river, but this time, he takes the sheep along. That way, he doesn't leave the sheep alone with the wolf (or the grain). Next, the farmer leaves the sheep alone and take the wolf (or the grain). He leaves the wolf alone with the grain on the other side of the river. The farmer then comes back for the sheep one last time. All three have now crossed the river successfully.

Puzzle #3 Mr. Jones' Math Class

Solution: If Mary speaks softer than Cindy but Josephine speaks more loudly than Cindy, then Mary speaks softer than Josephine. Hence, Mary will not be punished.

Puzzle #4 Speaking of Math Class...

Solution: The average score of the students who passed is 8. The average score of all 20 students is 6. So, 20 * 6 = 120. Next, the eight students that failed averaged 3. So, 8 * 3 = 24. After, subtracting the average score of those who failed from the class in total, 120 − 24 = 96. Finally, divide the remaining points among the number of students who passed (12). Thus, 96 / 12 = 8.

Puzzle #5 The Big Race in the City

Solution: The runners crossed the finish line as follows: B, C, D, A. The first runner to cross the finish line, and thus the champion, is B. Then, C arrives next. So, B, C... then D is between A and C. Thus, the order is B, C, D, A.

Puzzle #6 Going on Vacation With the Bros

Solution: Alex is neither flying nor driving. Since Jack is with Alex, he won't be driving or flying either (we can assume any other means of transport such as a train). Andy is flying. Since Charlie isn't going with Mike, who doesn't fly, then Andy and Charlie are going together by plane. That leaves Tom and Mike, who are planning to drive. Hence, Tom is going by car.

Puzzle #7 A Family of Big Eaters

Solution: Ace and Buddy eat more than Scout. Buddy eats less than Precious. Precious eats more than Ace, who, in turn, eats more than Scout. So, Scout eats the least of all four. This means he won't be put up for adoption like the other three.

Puzzle #8 To Shoplift or Not to Shoplift?

Solution: The lady is an employee of the store. She filled the shopping cart with materials that were not items for sale, for example, trash, and proceeded to take it outside. That is why the store's security did not stop her.

Puzzle #9 A Bit Too Much Excitement

Solution: The man is in a movie theater, hence the dark room. He took a drink and began choking on an ice cube. After a few moments, the ice cube melts, and the man is able to breathe and speak again.

Puzzle #10 Tell Me What You See

Solution: The answer to the code for a free premium membership is: "Reading between the lines" as the letters of the word "reading" have been placed in between lines.

Puzzle #11 Which Way Is Up?

Solution: The man is very short. So, he can reach the button for the lobby very easily, but cannot reach the button for the 45th floor in the evenings. (It is possible for him to just wait for someone taller to get on and push the button for him, but why wait when you can take the stairs?)

Puzzle #12 Going Around in Circles

Solution: She works in a large office building that has a circular parking tower. Her parking space is on the sixth floor of the parking tower. So, she needs to drive in circles six times before reaching her spot.

Puzzle #13 That's All She Wrote

Solution: This lady is a business owner. She is signing her name on the weekly paycheck of her 60 employees. Hence, she must do this every week, because everyone is counting on their weekly paycheck.

Puzzle #14 Swing and a Miss

Solution: As the batter swung at strike three, the ball got away from the catcher. Since the catcher lost control of the ball, the batter ran down to the first base and made it there safely before the catcher got the ball. Hence, the batter struck out but reached first base on the passed ball by the catcher.

Puzzle #15 Burning the Candle at Both Ends

Solution: Rob works at night. So, he is up all night at his job. Then, he gets home in the morning and sleeps all day. This is why he isn't exhausted in the morning, even after not sleeping at night.

Puzzle #16 Child's Play

Solution: After combining their sand piles, both kids have one large pile of sand.

Puzzle#17 Your Wishes Are My Command

Solution: The servant made the following request to his master: "My mother wishes to see her grandchild playing on a pile of gold." With this wish, the servant was able to combine all three wishes into a single one.

Puzzle #18 Something's Fishy

Solution: The vet felt sorry for the sweet lady. He couldn't imagine how devastated she would be if her beloved fish died. So, he replaced her dying pet fish with an identical, healthy one so the lady wouldn't notice the difference.

Puzzle #19 Final Destination

Solution: Bobby was a dog. He had chewed through the name tag that was put on his neck. That is why the railway staff was unable to figure out where he needed to go.

Puzzle #20 Someone Had to Draw the Line

Solution: Naturally, line "B" is longer. By circling "A," an optical illusion is created by simulating that "A" has been chosen as the longer line of the two. This is meant to determine if the test subjects would use their own perception even though an incorrect answer was suggested.

Puzzle #21 Swinging for the fences

Solution: The three horses that escaped the barn did not go very far, because the fence kept them inside the farmer's field. The other three horses stayed in the barn. This is why the farmer was able to find the three horses outside of the barn, but within the fence.

Puzzle #22 An Unusual Meal

Solution: Billy was one of the animals that had escaped from the zoo earlier in the day.

Puzzle #23 Where's the Dough?

Solution: The miser wanted to make sure that the bank had all of his money on hand. (Depending on the amount, though, the bank may not have that much cash on hand and may have to order it).

Puzzle #24 Going for a Ride

Solution: Since the wife took up more than one seat, the airline billed her for one and a half seats. Since the husband didn't even take up the entire seat, the airline decided to bill him for half a seat. In total, the couple was billed for two seats.

Puzzle #25 Paying the Price

Solution: The young lady was paying the fine on an overdue library book, and did not check out any additional books.

Puzzle #26 Not Buying It

Solution: Since the forecast was broadcast around midnight, the broadcast was wrong, as it would be nighttime in 72 hours. Hence, it would be impossible for it to be warm and sunny.

Puzzle #27 Life is a Game

Solution: Henry's father used the hammer to build a shelf in his room so high up that Henry couldn't reach it even if he pulled up a chair. So, Henry's father let him keep the console, but he couldn't play with it.

Puzzle #28 I Dare You

Solution: Mike jumped out of a window on the first floor. Since the window is only 3 feet off the ground, Mike was able to land safely on the street below, thereby fulfilling the dare.

Puzzle #29 What Are You Up To?

Solution: The robber was already in jail. The two officers came into his cell to take him to court to face trial. Hence, they didn't have to arrest him because he was already in custody.

Puzzle #30 It's Completely Puzzling…

Solution: The answer is 36.

To complete this puzzle, you must multiply the first two numbers in each row and then subtract the first digit from the result of the multiplication so that you can get the third number in that particular row.

So,

$(2 * 11) - 2 = 20$

$(4 * 9) - 4 = 32$

$(7 * 8) - 7 = 49$

$(4 * 10) - 4 = 36$

Hence, 36 is the correct answer to the puzzle.

Puzzle #31 Empty Space

Solution: The three men had, in fact, left the building. They went into the building to get a car from the parking garage and then drove away. (Alternatively, the men could have left through another exit, but this is unlikely as the security cameras did not pick them up walking out.)

Puzzle #32 Dude, I Can't Open the Door!

Solution: Since the man had been partying and drinking, his friends decided to take his car keys away. His house keys were on the same key ring. His friends then got this man a cab and sent him home without his keys. Hence, he was unable to enter his apartment without his keys.

Puzzle #33 What a Pile Up

Solution: The vehicles were toys. A child had been playing with them and piled up them on top of each other as a part of his game. The child had even tossed some of them around.

Puzzle #34 Whacky Weather

Solution: The man drove through a car wash. First, it was sunny, then dark, then the water came, then the wind picked up, and finally, the sun came back as he exited the car wash.

Puzzle #35 Are You Lion to Me?

Solution: The woman was unafraid and made no effort to flee because she was at a zoo, and the lion was located securely in its pen.

Puzzle #36 A Letter to the Editor

Solution: Dear reader, Regarding your letter where you posted a question, here is my reply: The letter "M" can be found once in a minute, twice in a moment but never in a hundred years. Best, the editor.

Puzzle #37 The Hitchhiker's Tale

Solution: The car was driverless because it had broken down. So, it was being pushed. The hitchhiker did not see the people pushing the car because of the heavy rain.

Puzzle #38 Some Legalese for You

Solution: Here is what the young lawyer said: Attempting suicide is punishable by law but cannot be punished if the individual takes their own life, as they are dead.

Puzzle #39 Mind your Ps and Qs

Solution: The correct answer is the word: DELETE. The 2nd, 4th, and 6th letters are "E." If you skip 7 letters starting from the first, you will get "L." Then, if you jump 7 letters again starting from the 3rd letter (L), you get "T."

Puzzle #40 Tunnel Vision

Solution: Since there is no other way around, and the height difference is only one inch, the driver has decided to deflate the tires just enough to fit under the top of the tunnel. Once through, the driver can then re-inflate the tires.

Puzzle #41 Now that You Mention It

Solution: The police officer did nothing about this situation because the truck driver was walking the wrong way on the one-way street. Hence, he was not breaking the law in any way.

Puzzle #42 Color me...

Solution: The bear was white. Since the man could only see south from all four corners of his home, he had to be atop the north pole. So, the only bears at the north pole are polar bears.

Puzzle #43 Making the Grade

Solution: The teacher instructed all of his students to raise their hands to answer every question. Those students who were sure they knew the right answer would raise their right hands. Those students who didn't know the answer would raise their left hand.

Hence, the teacher would be certain which students knew the right answer and which ones didn't.

Puzzle #44 The Fly in the Coffee

Solution: Even though the waiter had apparently gotten a fresh cup of coffee, the lady knew that it was the same cup of coffee but without the fly in it because she had already put sugar in it.

Puzzle #45 The All-Black

Solution: Even though everything is painted black and the man was completely dressed in black, the driver was able to see him because it was broad daylight.

Puzzle #46 A Job Interview

Solution: Since the job called for an exceptionally sharp candidate, the interview was impressed to see that the lady had understood his wordplay: T comes before U, that is, P Q R S T... U... V W X...

Puzzle #47 At Opposite Ends

Solution: The two colleagues cannot see each other because they are sitting with their back to each other.

Puzzle #48 Home Alone

Solution: You must light up the match first before you can light up anything else.

Puzzle #49 Happy Birthday

Solution: Only one! As a person can only have the same birthday every year.

Puzzle #50 Drawing the Line

Solution: To make the line shorter, draw a longer line next to it. Such as this:

Puzzle #51 Order in the Court

Solution: The judge denied the petition because it is impossible for a man to marry his widow's sister as he is already dead.

Puzzle #52 Driving me Crazy

Solution: Since you are the driver, the color of the driver's eyes is your own eye color.

Puzzle #53 A Man and his Daughters

Solution: Jennifer's dad's first four daughters have already been named. So, Jennifer's dad's fifth daughter's name is Jennifer.

Puzzle #54 A Traffic Jam

Solution: As long as your car is any color that isn't blue, green, red, or yellow, you are free to circulate any day of the week.

Puzzle #55 At the Mercy of the Court

Solution: For the felon to save his life, he has to choose the second door, because the lions have already been starved to death after not eating for four years.

Puzzle #56 Oh My Son!

Solution: The surgeon about to perform the operation was the son's mother.

Puzzle #57 Challenge Me!

Solution: The caller named the following three consecutive days: Yesterday, today and tomorrow.

Puzzle #58 Out the Window

Solution: While the window washer was cleaning the windows on the 35th floor, he was cleaning the inside of windows. So, his fall only resulted in a bruised ego.

Puzzle #59 Make Sure You Study for the Test

Solution: The only word in the English language that maintains the same pronunciation even after four of its five letters have been removed is QUEUE.

Puzzle #60 A Cat's Meow

Solution: The side of a cat that has the most hair is the outside of the cat.

Puzzle #61 Do What You Will

Solution: The lawyer indicated that the man could not be buried in Texas because he was still alive. He needed to die first before he could be buried in Texas. Hence, the will would have to state something like, "Upon my passing, it is my will to be buried in Texas."

Now that you have seen the solutions to the puzzles, please don't spoil them! Give yourself a chance to work out each of the puzzles. Once you have reached an answer, then you can have a look at the solution.

Once you have seen the solution to a puzzle, try to see if there is another possible solution to the problem. The chances are that there is another possible solution to the problem without it being too wacky or too "out there."

Please keep the following concept in mind: The simplest answer is usually the right one.

So, take your time. Go through each item, and make sure you work out all of the possible solutions in your mind before you arrive at a conclusion.

Conclusion

Thanks again for purchasing this book. It was created with the intent to get your creative juices flowing and have some fun at the same time. Please take the time to go over each of these puzzles and figure out the best possible solutions for each one.

Once you have gone through each of the puzzles, you can lead your own sessions. You can get your friends, families, and colleagues to work on each of these puzzles while you lead the discussion. Your experience will certainly be useful in helping others get the most out of each one

In fact, it is always fun to speculate on alternative solutions. Often, you will find that thinking outside the box can lead to some wonderful discussion and debate. After all, creative thinking is all about finding alternate solutions to common, everyday situations. So, don't hold back. Do take the time to explore other possibilities.

If you liked this book, do check out the others in this series. You will find them to be just as fun and interesting. They will definitely provide you with hours of fun and entertainment.

As always, if you have found this book to be fun and interesting, don't forget to leave a comment. Other readers who are interested in picking up a book such as this will greatly appreciate your honest opinion.

Hopefully, they will be able to get as much enjoyment out of this book as you have.

Thanks again.

See you next time!

Connect with us on our Facebook page www.facebook.com/bluesourceandfriends and stay tuned to our latest book promotions and free giveaways.

Printed in Great Britain
by Amazon